D0867005

DECLARATION

•

I hereby declare that
all the paper produced
by Cartiere del Garda S.p.A.
in its Riva del Garda mill
is manufactured completely
Acid-free and Wood-free

Dr. Alois Lueftinger
Managing Director and General Manager
Cartiere del Garda S.p.A.

GREEN WORLD

FLOWERING PLANTS

Written by
Wendy Madgwick

STECK-VAUGHN
L I B R A R Y
A Division of Steck-Vaughn Company
Austin, Texas

**Published in the United States in 1990
by Steck-Vaughn, Co., Austin, Texas,**
a subsidiary of National Education Corporation

A Templar Book
Devised and produced by The Templar Company plc
Pippbrook Mill, London Road, Dorking, Surrey RH4 1JE, Great Britain
Copyright © 1990 by The Templar Company plc

Editor: Wendy Madgwick
Designer: Jane Hunt
Illustrators: David Ashby and Sallie Reason

Notes to Reader
There are some words in this book that are printed in **bold** type.
A brief explanation of these words is given in the glossary on p. 44.

All living things are given two Latin names when first classified by a
scientist. Some of them also have a common name, for example the meadow
buttercup, *Ranunculus acris*. In this book, the common name is used where
possible, but the scientific name is given when first mentioned.

This book deals mainly with herbaceous (non-woody) flowering plants.
Other flowering plants are covered in other books in the series.

Library of Congress Cataloging-in-Publication Data
Madgwick, Wendy, 1946–
Flowering plants / by Wendy Madgwick.   p. cm. – (The Green World)
"A Templar Book" – T.p. verso.   Includes bibliographical references.
Summary: Surveys the world of flowering plants, discussing such aspects
as plant growth, reproduction, pollination, flowers, seeds, fruits, lost
habitats, and the extinction of plants.
ISBN 0-8114-2730-7
1. Plants – Juvenile literature.   2. Angiosperms – Juvenile literature.
[1. Angiosperms.   2. Plants.]   I. Title.   II. Series.
QK49.M317   1990   90-9572
582.13–dc20   CIP AC

Color separations by Positive Colour Ltd, Maldon, Essex, Great Britain
Printed and bound by L.E.G.O., Vicenza, Italy
1 2 3 4 5 6 7 8 9 0 LE 94 93 92 91 90

Photographic credits
t = top, b = bottom, l = left, r = right
Cover: Bruce Coleman; page 9 Bruce Coleman/L.C. Marigo; page 10
Frank Lane/P. Kirkpatrick; page 11 Frank Lane/Michael Rose; page 12
Bruce Coleman/J. Langsbury; page 14 Frank Lane/M. Withers; page 17
Bruce Coleman/S.J. Krasemann; page 21 Frank Lane/Eric & David Hosking;
page 23 Frank Lane/Eric & David Hosking; page 24 Bruce Coleman/
E. Crichton; page 26 Bruce Coleman/N. Devore III; page 28 Bruce Coleman/
J. Burton; page 29 Frank Lane/R. Tidman; page 33*t* Frank Lane/Eric &
David Hosking; page 33*b* Spectrum; page 35 Bruce Coleman/A. Compost;
page 40 Bruce Coleman/M. Viard; page 41 Frank Lane/B. Henry;
page 43 Malaysian Rubber Producers Research Association.

CONTENTS

GREEN WORLD

This tree shows the different groups of plants that are found in the world. It does not show how they developed or their relationship with each other.

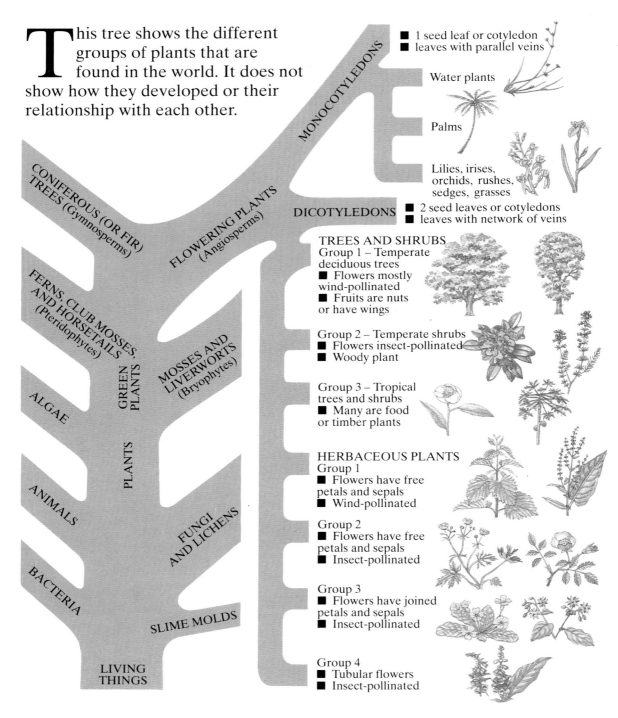

MONOCOTYLEDONS
- 1 seed leaf or cotyledon
- leaves with parallel veins

Water plants

Palms

Lilies, irises, orchids, rushes, sedges, grasses

DICOTYLEDONS
- 2 seed leaves or cotyledons
- leaves with network of veins

TREES AND SHRUBS
Group 1 – Temperate deciduous trees
- Flowers mostly wind-pollinated
- Fruits are nuts or have wings

Group 2 – Temperate shrubs
- Flowers insect-pollinated
- Woody plant

Group 3 – Tropical trees and shrubs
- Many are food or timber plants

HERBACEOUS PLANTS
Group 1
- Flowers have free petals and sepals
- Wind-pollinated

Group 2
- Flowers have free petals and sepals
- Insect-pollinated

Group 3
- Flowers have joined petals and sepals
- Insect-pollinated

Group 4
- Tubular flowers
- Insect-pollinated

CONIFEROUS (OR FIR) TREES (Gymnosperms)

FLOWERING PLANTS (Angiosperms)

FERNS, CLUB MOSSES, AND HORSETAILS (Pteridophytes)

MOSSES AND LIVERWORTS (Bryophytes)

GREEN PLANTS

ALGAE

PLANTS

FUNGI AND LICHENS

ANIMALS

BACTERIA

SLIME MOLDS

LIVING THINGS

The land area of the world is divided into ten main zones depending on the plants that grow there. The only place that flowering plants cannot grow is in the permanently frozen Antarctic.

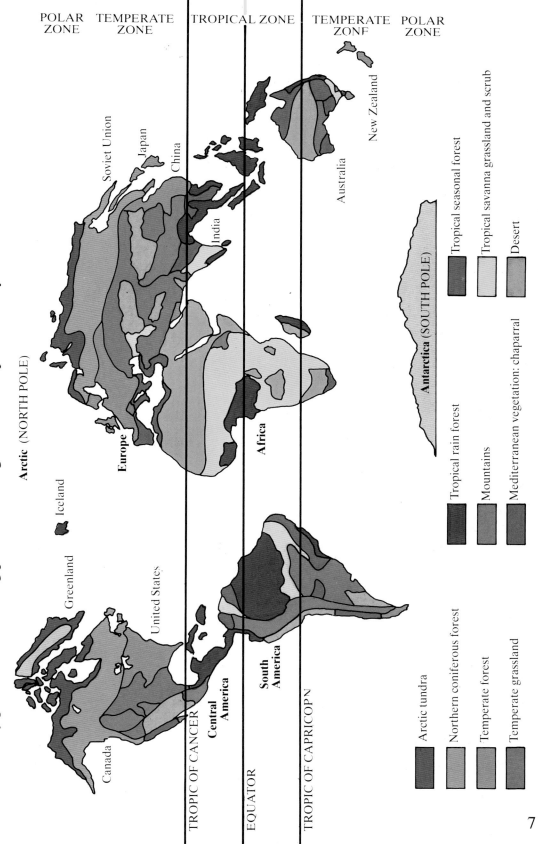

POLAR ZONE · TEMPERATE ZONE · TROPICAL ZONE · TEMPERATE ZONE · POLAR ZONE

Arctic (NORTH POLE)

Iceland
Greenland
Canada
United States
Soviet Union
Japan
China
India
Europe
Africa
Central America
South America
Australia
New Zealand

TROPIC OF CANCER
EQUATOR
TROPIC OF CAPRICORN

Antarctica (SOUTH POLE)

Arctic tundra
Northern coniferous forest
Temperate forest
Temperate grassland

Tropical rain forest
Mountains
Mediterranean vegetation: chaparral

Tropical seasonal forest
Tropical savanna grassland and scrub
Desert

7

FLOWERING PLANTS

There are more flowering plants or **angiosperms** on the Earth than any other kind. They include garden flowers (herbaceous or nonwoody plants), shrubs, and trees as well as climbing vines, grasses, and cacti. Most of them have roots and a stem, which support the leaves and flowers. The flowers come in all shapes and colors, but they all have the same function. They produce the male sex cells, protected in **pollen grains**, and the female sex cells or **ovules** (see p. 20). When these cells fuse or join together, a **seed** is formed that will grow into the new plant (see p. 26). It is these specialized flowers that have allowed plants to adapt or change so that they can survive nearly everywhere on Earth.

This book will cover the general biology of flowering plants, but will look mainly at herbaceous plants throughout the world.

From the tropics to the poles

Flowering plants come in so many shapes and sizes because the areas and conditions in which they live are so varied. They are found in hot, dry deserts, in the cold Arctic, in lakes and marshes, high up on mountains, and in the forests and grasslands of both temperate and tropical areas (see the map on page 7).

the Arctic saxifrage (*Saxifraga nivalis*) grows close to the ground

the sea aster (*Aster tripolium*) grows in salt marshes

the giant saguaro (*Carnegiea gigantea*) cactus reaches a height of 45 feet

the passion flower (*Passiflora* species) of Brazil is a climbing vine

One leaf or two?

Flowering plants are divided into two main groups: dicotyledons and monocotyledons. Dicotyledons have two seed leaves or cotyledons and the leaves often have a network of veins. They include such plants as poppies, woodland trees, and cabbages. Monocotyledons have only one cotyledon and the veins run in straight lines along the length of the leaf. They include grasses, lilies, rushes, sedges, bananas, and orchids.

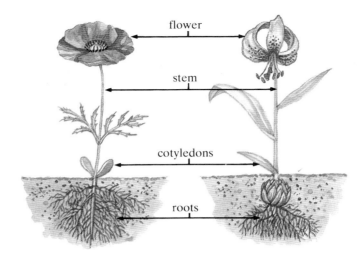

flower

stem

cotyledons

roots

■ Flowering plants or angiosperms produce seeds that grow inside a fruit.
■ They are usually green plants which make their own food by **photosynthesis** from carbon dioxide, a gas, and water using the energy of sunlight (see p. 16).
■ They are the largest group of plants with at least 255,000 species.
■ They are divided into two main groups: dicotyledons and monocotyledons.
■ They have roots, stems, and leaves.

One year or many?

Many plants grow, flower, produce seeds, and die all in one season – they are **annuals**. **Biennials** start to grow one year then flower, seed, and die the next. Plants that live for many years and flower each year are called **perennials**. A few tropical plants such as bromeliads (see below: *Tillandsia stricta*) and puyas live for several years but only flower and seed once. When eight to ten years old, the Jamaican mountain pride (*Spathelia* species) makes a huge cluster of bright red flowers up to 5 feet high and 7 1/2 feet across. When the seeds are ripe, the plant dies.

the Alpine columbine (*Aquilegia* species) is a rare flower of the Alps

the Japanese cherry tree (*Prunus* species)

ALL OVER THE WORLD

In order to grow and flourish, plants need soil, light, water, and a long enough growing season to produce flowers and seeds. If you look at the map on page 7, you will see that it is indeed a green world. Only the permanently frozen areas of the Antarctic and the deep salt oceans do not support flowering plants. Some plants are so adaptable that they can live in many different areas but most are specialized and can only grow in one particular kind of area or habitat. Each of the main areas in which plants live have their own special problems, and the plants that live there have overcome these in various and unique ways.

Desert plants

Over a third of the Earth's surface is covered by desert or semidesert. Deserts are found in Africa, Asia, Australia, and the Americas. Some, like the Kalahari desert in Africa, are very hot but in others, for example the Mojave desert in California, it gets cold enough to snow. The thing they have in common is lack of water.

Deserts often appear to be very barren places with only a few plants dotting the sandy wastelands, but if you could look beneath the sand you would see a jungle of roots growing out in search of water. Cacti and similar plants are "drought resisters." They store water in their fleshy stems and their leaves often have become protective spines. Others are short-lived "drought evaders." They come up after rain, and flower, set seed, and die in the space of a few days. When this happens, as above in the Mojave desert, the desert "blooms."

Woodland plants

Deciduous woodlands with broadleaved trees that lose their leaves in autumn are the main kind of vegetation found in temperate regions. However, many woods have been cut down to make room for farms, houses, and industry. On a walk through a temperate forest you will see many flowering plants from the tall trees, like birch and oak that tower above your head, to the small wood violets and wood anemones beneath your feet. Plants that live on the forest floor often grow and flower in spring, before the trees are in full leaf and cut off too much light.

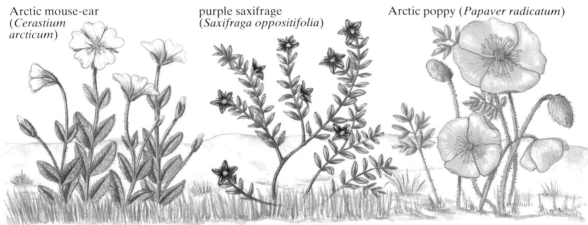

Arctic mouse-ear (*Cerastium arcticum*)

purple saxifrage (*Saxifraga oppositifolia*)

Arctic poppy (*Papaver radicatum*)

Flowers of the snow

No flowering plants can survive in areas that are permanently frozen, and trees can only survive in the less-cold regions of the Arctic. Arctic flowers are often small, growing close to the ground for protection from the strong winds and to stop them from losing heat. Their leaves have tough, waxy skins or are covered in fine hairs to protect them from the cold and the bright sunlight reflected off the snow. Large supplies of food in their roots help them to survive in severe weather, and many Arctic plants make new plants by sending out runners or underground shoots. The flowers are relatively big, like the Arctic poppy which has large bowl-shaped flowers. These trap sunlight, which makes them warm, and tempts insects to visit them.

PLANT LIFE

Without plants, the world as we know it could not exist. Plants form the basis on which most other living things depend. Most animals, including humans, depend on flowering plants for food, particularly grasses such as rice and grain. Everywhere on Earth, plants and animals depend on each other for survival. Many flowers need insects to pollinate them and the insects could not survive without the pollen and sugary **nectar** as food. **Succulent** or juicy-leaved desert plants provide water, shade, and shelter for desert animals.

In woods and forests the trees provide food products or nutrients for the soil as well as food for animals and the oxygen we breathe (see p. 16). Grasses, trees, and shrubs develop massive rooting systems that anchor the soil and stop it from being blown or washed away. When plants die or shed their leaves, they decompose and their remains form humus which helps to make the soil more fertile.

Grasslands

There are two main types of grassland, tropical savannas and temperate grasslands. Many temperate grasslands have been plowed to grow crops or hay. If the grass in a meadow is not cut regularly, wild flowers like cowslips (*Primula* species), meadowsweet (*Filipendula ulmaria*), and field poppies (*Papaver rhoeas*), grow (see below).

The most common or dominant plants of savannas are the tall grasses such as elephant and rooigrass. Trees such as the flat-topped acacias, baobabs, and tamarind can also be seen.

Plants of the tropics

Tropical rain forests have taken thousands of years to grow and develop. They are found in the Amazon basin of South America, in southern Asia, parts of Australia, and in the central zone of Africa. They are the powerhouses of the world, soaking up vast amounts of rain water and recycling it. They also take in tons of carbon dioxide and pump out masses of oxygen during photosynthesis (see p. 16). About 50 percent of all flowering plants are found in rain forests and new ones are being discovered daily.

Trees tower to the skies, but few plants can grow on the dark forest floor. Orchids and lianas, or vines, scramble over the trees in their search for light. They are **epiphytes**, or air plants, taking moisture and food from the air. Plants like *Rafflesia* are **parasites**, living on other plants (see p. 38). Others feed on insects and are **carnivores** (see p. 36). Indian pipes are **saprophytes**, feeding on decaying animals and plants.

Mountains

Mountains are always exposed to wind and cold as well as enormous changes in temperature. Trees grow at the foot of most mountains but higher up the trees die out and other plants take over. All mountain flowers grow close to the ground and, as they often have short growing seasons, they flower and seed quickly. The soil is often poor and so the plants grow slowly and have large rooting systems. Most are perennials (see p. 9), and live for a long time. Many plants flourish on the slopes of the Alps. Typical mountain flowers include the stemless blue gentian (*Gentiana nivalis*), wild tulips (*Tulipa sylvestris*), and narcissus (*Narcissus* species).

ROOTS AND SHOOTS

Although the flowering plants include such different plants as trees, daisies, and grasses, they are all formed in the same way. They all have a root and stem, which carries the leaves and flowers. The stem and leaves together are called the shoot, and the roots and the shoots work together. The roots need the shoots to make them food, and the shoots need the roots to provide them with water and minerals. If a plant's roots are damaged, the plant will die. The basic structure of a typical flowering plant is shown opposite.

Tall or short?
The tallest flowering plants with the longest stems are trees. However, some plants that only grow for one season and then die back can also be quite tall. The tallest is the giant hogweed from Asia (*Heracleum mantegazzianum*) whose stem can reach up to 15 feet. At the other extreme, the chaffweed (*Anagallis minima*) is only inches high.

Roots galore
Roots have many functions. Some store food (see p. 41) and others, for instance those of grasses, produce a mass of branching roots that help to bind the soil. Plants in dry areas grow long tap roots in search of water. Many tropical trees such as figs produce thin buttress roots high up their trunks. These act like guy-ropes, helping to anchor the shallow-rooted trees in the soil.

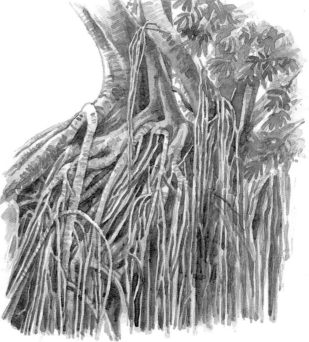

Transportation Systems

In humans, digested food is carried around the body in the blood. In plants, nutrients are dissolved in water and carried in a vast system of very tiny tubes that reach from the tips of the roots to the tips of the leaves. They can be seen as the veins in leaves.

There are two sets of tubes, which run side by side up the plant. The **phloem** tubes carry food from the leaves all around the plant. In spring, food stored in the roots is carried up to the growing shoots. **Xylem** tubes work like drinking straws. The leaves are covered with tiny holes called **stomata**, and the water in the leaves evaporates or turns into water vapor, a gas, which passes out through these holes. As the water evaporates, it pulls more water up the xylem from the roots, just as water moves up a straw when you suck it. The stomata can open and close, so if it is very dry and too much water is being lost they close. If it is hot, they open; water lost through the leaves helps to cool the plant. Xylem tubes are hard and woody. They help to keep the stem stiff and straight and the leaves firm and spread out to catch the light.

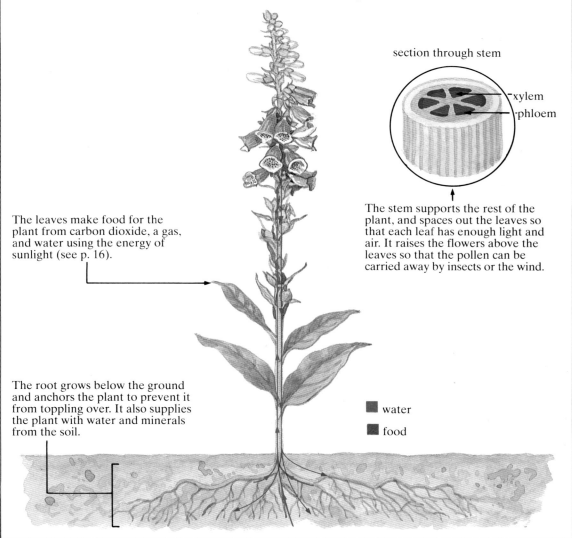

section through stem

xylem

phloem

The stem supports the rest of the plant, and spaces out the leaves so that each leaf has enough light and air. It raises the flowers above the leaves so that the pollen can be carried away by insects or the wind.

The leaves make food for the plant from carbon dioxide, a gas, and water using the energy of sunlight (see p. 16).

The root grows below the ground and anchors the plant to prevent it from toppling over. It also supplies the plant with water and minerals from the soil.

■ water

■ food

HOW PLANTS GROW

The leaves are the "food factories" of plants: they make new living plant material from simple, nonliving chemicals. When a house is built from bricks, a lot of energy is needed by the builder to lift the bricks and cement them together. Plants also need energy to combine simple chemicals into more complex materials. This energy comes from sunlight (see below).

When animals grow, they grow all over at the same time, so they stay more or less the same shape. Most plants, however, grow only at the tips of the shoots and roots and they often change their shape as new buds sprout to produce side branches. If the plant is shaded, it may grow in a curve toward the light. If it is exposed to strong winds, it may grow twisted and bent.

The Miracle of Photosynthesis

The leaves trap energy from light to use for growth. A leaf's green color comes from a special pigment called **chlorophyll**. The chlorophyll, contained in special cells called chloroplasts, absorbs light and uses the light's energy to make food.

The surface of the leaf is covered with tiny stomata, almost too small to see, which allow air to enter. The roots supply the leaves with water and minerals from the soil. The leaf uses the energy from sunlight to join together carbon dioxide gas from the air and water from the soil to make a simple sugar called glucose. This process is called photosynthesis, which means "joining with light." The glucose can then be changed into other materials, including starch, fats, and cellulose. It can also join up with minerals such as nitrates and phosphates to make proteins and amino acids.

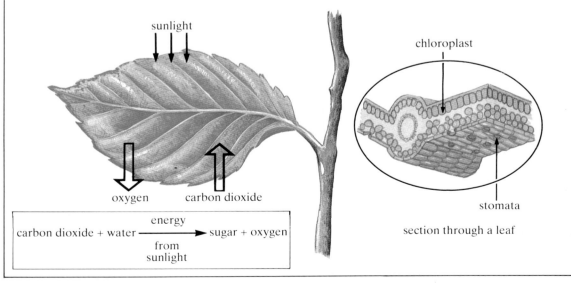

sunlight

oxygen   carbon dioxide

chloroplast

stomata

section through a leaf

$$\text{carbon dioxide} + \text{water} \xrightarrow[\substack{\text{from} \\ \text{sunlight}}]{\text{energy}} \text{sugar} + \text{oxygen}$$

Grow, grow, grow!

All animals stop growing once they reach a certain size – mice never grow as large as elephants, and even elephants stop growing as adults. Plants can keep on growing all their lives. The largest plant in the world – indeed, the largest living thing in the world – is the giant sequoia tree. The tallest flowering tree, the Australian mountain ash (*Eucalyptus regnons*, pictured here), is 345 feet high. Trees can reach this size because they live for hundreds of years.

A time to grow

In the lush tropical jungle, plants can grow every day, but in the far north some plants may be able to grow for only six weeks of the year, in the middle of summer. They grow extremely slowly and never get very big, like the plants in the Arctic pictured here. In temperate areas that have cold winters, there is a great burst of growth in spring, when the temperature rises and the days grow longer.

SPECIAL LEAVES

Have you noticed how many different kinds of leaves there are? Dandelion leaves are long and jagged, daisy leaves are round and smooth, and holly leaves are shiny and prickly. Some leaves have stalks and others have none. Some leaves are very simple and each leaf is joined to the stem by its own stalk. Other leaves are made up of several small leaves or leaflets, all joined to the same stalk.

The leaf veins can form patterns, and the type of pattern depends on which group the plant belongs to. In dicotyledons, the leaf veins form a net with the veins all linked together. In monocotyledons, the veins run in parallel lines along the length of the leaf. The veins in a leaf carry food and water and also help to support the soft parts of the leaf.

The outer surface of a leaf contains a waxy material called cutin. It stops too much water from being lost from the leaf surface and helps to protect the leaf. Very woolly leaves also save water as the water vapor cannot get past the thick mat of hairs.

Floating leaves

Water lilies live in ponds and lakes, where they float at the water's surface. Their leaves are spongy and filled with air, which helps to keep them afloat. Duckweeds have very small leaves with little spongy bags of air underneath.

water lilies (*Nymphaea* species)

duckweeds (*Lemna* species)

Desert plants

In hot, dry climates, water evaporates quickly from the leaves, and plants are in danger of wilting and dying. Many desert plants have fat, juicy leaves whose cells store water. Fat, round leaves have a much smaller surface area than wide leaves, so they are less likely to lose water.

Cacti are full of water and very juicy and are a welcome source of food and water for desert animals. To stop animals from eating them, cactus leaves do not look like leaves. Instead they are stiff, sharp spikes that can inflict a nasty wound. To make up for "losing" their leaves, cacti use their fat green stems for photosynthesis.

Climbers and scramblers

Some plants use their leaves for climbing. The clematis has very weak stems, and relies on scrambling up other plants in order to reach the light. The leaf stalks can feel when they touch a support, and they twine around it. Pea leaves use curling tendrils at the tips of their leaves for twining around supports.

Brambles and wild roses also scramble over other plants. They have backward pointing thorns on their stems and leaves, which act like little grappling hooks. Goosegrass has even tinier hooks that you can hardly see. Its leaves, stems, and fruits catch and cling to your clothes as you brush past them.

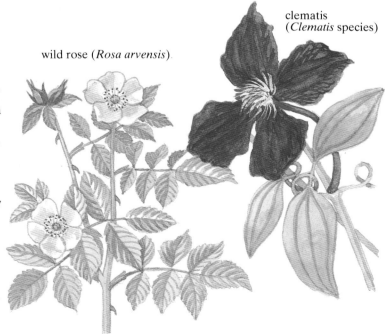

clematis (*Clematis* species)

wild rose (*Rosa arvensis*)

19

HOW FLOWERS REPRODUCE

The flowers are often the first thing you notice about a plant. Even the simple buttercup looks like a work of art. The bright colors and amazing shapes are all for one purpose: to attract a pollinator to take the pollen from one plant to another.

The transfer of pollen from a male **anther** to a female **stigma** is called **pollination**. When a pollen grain lands on a stigma, the male cell from the pollen grain penetrates the stigma and grows down the **style** to the **ovary**. In a process called sexual reproduction, the male cell **fertilizes** or fuses with the ovule to form a seed. Under suitable conditions a seed will **germinate** (begin to grow) and develop into a new plant (see p. 30). The ovary swells to form a fruit which protects the seeds (see p. 27).

Structure of a flower
Flowers differ according to where they grow, the soil they grow on, and the climate they grow in, but they all have the same basic structure.

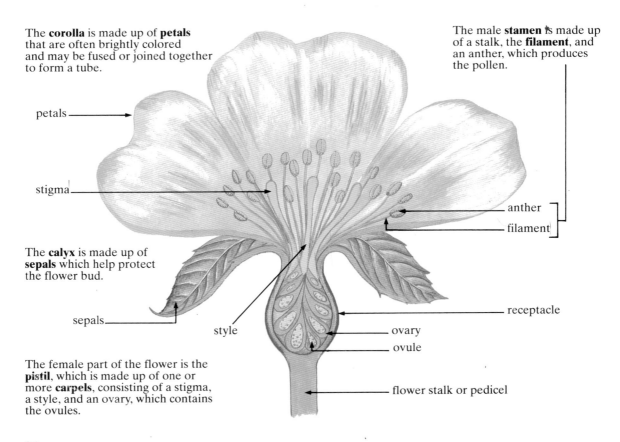

The **corolla** is made up of **petals** that are often brightly colored and may be fused or joined together to form a tube.

The male **stamen** is made up of a stalk, the **filament**, and an anther, which produces the pollen.

petals

stigma

anther

filament

The **calyx** is made up of **sepals** which help protect the flower bud.

sepals

style

ovary

ovule

receptacle

flower stalk or pedicel

The female part of the flower is the **pistil**, which is made up of one or more **carpels**, consisting of a stigma, a style, and an ovary, which contains the ovules.

Color, scent, and nectar

Sexual reproduction is the main function of the flower but the most noticeable parts are usually the petals. In many plants, the petals are brightly colored and scented to attract insects that transfer the pollen from flower to flower. Pollen is a valuable food for insects as it is rich in protein. The petals also produce a sweet, sugary liquid called nectar which animals also eat. In some flowers like clematis and winter aconite (*Eranthis hyemalis*) the sepals instead of the petals are colored. In the winter aconite, pictured here, the petals form a long, tube-shaped nectary that makes a great deal of nectar.

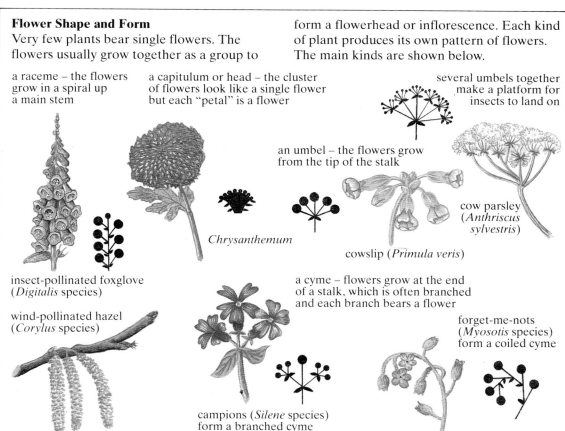

Flower Shape and Form

Very few plants bear single flowers. The flowers usually grow together as a group to form a flowerhead or inflorescence. Each kind of plant produces its own pattern of flowers. The main kinds are shown below.

a raceme – the flowers grow in a spiral up a main stem

a capitulum or head – the cluster of flowers look like a single flower but each "petal" is a flower

several umbels together make a platform for insects to land on

an umbel – the flowers grow from the tip of the stalk

Chrysanthemum

cowslip (*Primula veris*)

cow parsley (*Anthriscus sylvestris*)

insect-pollinated foxglove (*Digitalis* species)

wind-pollinated hazel (*Corylus* species)

a cyme – flowers grow at the end of a stalk, which is often branched and each branch bears a flower

forget-me-nots (*Myosotis* species) form a coiled cyme

campions (*Silene* species) form a branched cyme

POLLINATION

The transfer of pollen from one flower to another is very important. However, the chance of a pollen grain reaching the stigma of the right plant is so small that millions of pollen grains must be produced. Pollen grains come in all shapes and sizes, each one special to a particular plant. This makes sure that only pollen from the same kind of plant can fertilize the ovule. The process of pollination and fertilization is shown below.

Most flowering plants produce both male and female parts on the same flower, that is they are hermaphrodites. If pollen from the anther lands on the stigma of the same plant then **self-pollination** and **self-fertilization** occurs. If the pollen is from another plant, then **cross-pollination** and **cross-fertilization** occurs. Cross-pollination produces offspring that are different from the parent and so they may be able to live in different conditions. This means the plants may stand a better chance of spreading to other areas.

Pollination and fertilization
The pollen grains land on the stigma and tubes grow down to the ovary. The male cells fertilize the ovules which develop into the seeds.

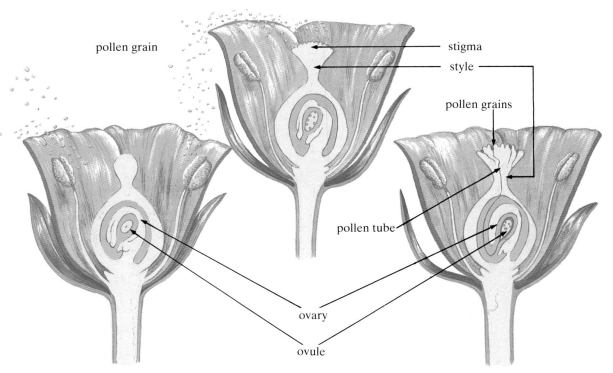

pollen grain

stigma

style

pollen grains

pollen tube

ovary

ovule

Animal pollination

Many flowers are pollinated by insects, although in the tropics birds and bats are also important. These plants usually have large, colorful, scented flowers with a lot of pollen and nectar, valuable food for the animals. As the animal brushes against the stamen, the rough or sticky pollen will stick to its body. When the animals then brush against the stigma of another plant the pollen may be transferred. Many petals have patterns, markings, or color changes that act as guidelines to insects leading them into the center of the flower.

Wind pollination

Most wind-pollinated plants such as grasses, sedges, rushes, and some trees have small flowers with tiny petals and sepals. The anthers are at the ends of long filaments, which move easily in the wind, and the pollen grains are small and light. The stigmas are large and feathery to trap the pollen. The flowers are often unisexual containing either male or female parts.

Aids to cross-pollination

To prevent self-pollination, the stigma of many plants matures after the anther. In others the plants bear either all male or female flowers. Primroses produce two types of plants: one with pin-eyed flowers and the other with thrum-eyed. The pollen produced by pin-eyed flowers can only pollinate thrum-eyed flowers and vice-versa, so cross-pollination is ensured.

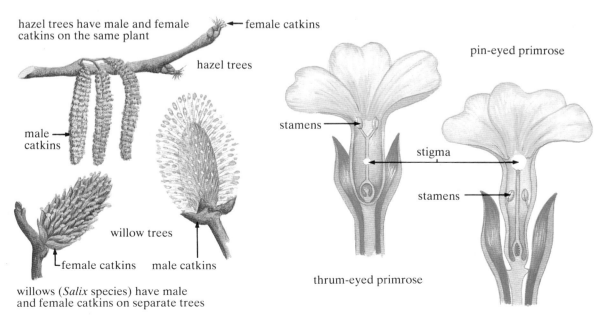

hazel trees have male and female catkins on the same plant

female catkins

hazel trees

male catkins

willow trees

female catkins   male catkins

willows (*Salix* species) have male and female catkins on separate trees

pin-eyed primrose

stamens

stigma

stamens

thrum-eyed primrose

SPECIAL FLOWERS

Simple flowers like poppies attract and are pollinated by all kinds of insects. In their struggle to survive and ensure pollination, many plants have developed flowers that can only be pollinated by particular kinds of animals. For instance, teasels (*Dipsacus fullonum*) catch pools of water in their cupped leaves and so stop ants, which are too small to be good pollinators, from reaching the flowers. The foxglove has a mass of fine hairs in the flower tube that stops small insects from entering. In toadflax (*Linaria* species) and many orchids the petal tubes are closed so that only a heavy insect can force its way in.

The very fragrant butterfly orchids and honeysuckles are pollinated by butterflies and night-flying moths. Their pale colors and strong scent make them easy to find at night and their nectar at the end of a long corolla tube can only be reached by long-tongued insects.

Hummingbirds, with their long, curved beaks, feed on the nectar of plants like fuchsias. Plants and birds have gradually adapted so that each kind of plant has its own special bird pollinator. When the habitats of these flowers are destroyed, the birds are lost, too.

Animal mimics

Orchids are a fascinating group of plants. Many tropical species have developed complex flowers that look like dolls or insects. The insect mimics look like flies or wasps with parts that resemble heads, feelers, and wings. It has been shown that, given the choice, male wasps prefer mating with fly orchids than with female wasps! Other orchids not only look like furry bees, they also smell like them. Once again the male bee pollinates the flower as it tries to mate with it.

Fly traps

Plants like the stinking hellebore (*Helleborus foetidus*) and carrion plants attract flies with their smell of rotting meat. Tropical arums lure insects into their flowers by the smell and warmth, which is produced by the spadix (the dark part in the middle of the flower). Once inside, the fly is trapped. Backward-pointing hairs stop the fly from getting out again. When ripe, the stamens burst open, covering the fly in pollen. Now the hairs die back, and the fly can escape, only to fly away to another arum flower. The giant flower of Sumatra (*Amorphophallus titanum*) is over 6 feet tall and gives off a foul smell that attracts carrion beetles to pollinate it.

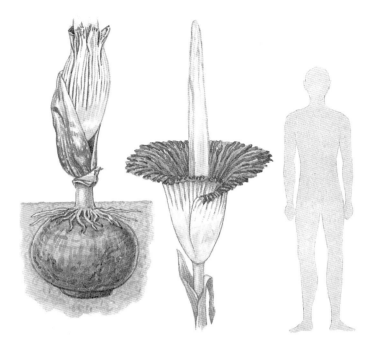

Water plants

Living in water poses a problem for plants – how to ensure pollination. Insect-pollinated flowers are often long-stemmed with their roots in the soil and the leaves and flowers held high above the water. Other plants float on the surface and they can be wind- or water-pollinated like pondweeds, or have cup-shaped, insect-pollinated flowers like water lilies. Others like the Canadian pondweed and hornwort grow beneath the water. The ripe anthers float to the surface of the water where the pollen is released. The pollen sinks and lands on and fertilizes the submerged stigma.

water iris
(*Iris pseudacorus*)

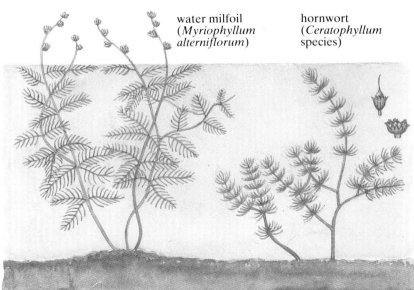

water milfoil
(*Myriophyllum alterniflorum*)

hornwort
(*Ceratophyllum* species)

SEEDS AND FRUITS

At the end of flowering, the petals wither and die, and the fertilized ovules develop into seeds. A seed contains the **embryo** of the new plant, waiting and ready to grow. Seeds are surrounded by a tough coat or testa. Some also contain a store of food – the **endosperm**. This is particularly large in grasses and cereal plants. Other plants, for instance peas and beans, store food in the cotyledons.

The number of seeds produced by a flower varies enormously. Usually large numbers are made but occasionally only one large seed is produced. The seeds are enclosed in a fruit that helps to protect the seeds and ensure that they are spread away from the parent plant. The fruits form and develop in a variety of ways. Some are very simple and contain only one seed, while others are complex or fleshy and contain many seeds (see opposite).

Large or small?

The size and number of seeds made by a plant depends on many things, but usually the more competition there is for food, space, and light, the larger the seed. Large seeds with a good food supply ensure the survival of the young plant, but few new plants are produced. The largest known seed is the double coconut from the Seychelles, which weighs 20 to 40 pounds. Orchids produce thousands of dustlike seeds the smallest of which, the creeping lady's tresses orchid (*Goodyera repens*), is only 2 micrograms. (A microgram is one millionth of a gram.)

Fruits for All Occasions

The fruits are adapted in shape according to the way in which they are dispersed (see the next page). There are two major types, dry and succulent or fleshy. The main kinds in each group are shown below.

DRY FRUITS

Achenes
■ Simple fruits with dry fruit walls; contain one seed.
■ Fruit walls have hooks, feathers, or wings.
■ Some, like nuts, have thickened fruit walls.
■ The fruits do not burst open (they are indehiscent).

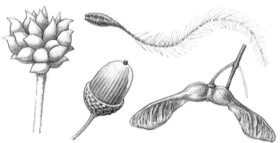

Capsules
■ Made up of several ovaries fused together.
■ Contain many seeds.
■ Fruits open by holes or slits.
■ Seeds are either shaken out or thrown out when the fruit bursts open (they are dehiscent).

Legumes and follicles
■ Formed from single ovary.
■ Contain many seeds.
■ Split along one (follicles) or two (legumes) sides.
■ Seeds either fall out or are shot out when pods burst open.

SOFT FRUITS

Drupes and Drupules
■ Ovary wall is thick and fleshy.
■ Contain a single seed.
■ Seed often inside a hard stone formed from the ovary wall.
■ Fruit sometimes made from many small drupes called drupules (for example, blackberries).

Berries
■ Fruit is more than one ovary fused together.
■ Seeds are not surrounded by a stone.
■ May contain one seed (dates) or many (bananas, tomato, gooseberry).

False fruits
■ Fleshy fruit is not the ovary but another part of the flower such as the receptacle.
■ The seed are either in a core (apples) or on the outside of the fruit (strawberries).
■ The seeds are not inside a stone.

SPREADING SEEDS

In order to grow into a new plant, a seed needs space, light, food, and water. If there are too many other plants around, the seed may begin to grow but the seedling may not survive. Flowering plants have developed many ways of making sure that they survive and spread to new areas. It is one reason why they are so successful.

There are four main ways in which seeds are carried to a new site – by wind, animals, water, or by explosion of the fruit. The method used depends on the type of seed and fruit produced (see p. 27).

Blown by the wind

Many plants have modified fruit that can be blown by the wind. Orchids have tiny seeds that are spread by the merest breeze, while other larger seeds need help to float. Sycamore seeds have wings and can travel up to 2 1/2 miles. Others have developed hairy "parachutes," which give them lift and help them float. The dandelion (*Taraxacum* species) "clocks" pictured here can be carried up to 30 feet.

Going off with a bang!

Many dry seeds explode when they are ripe, shooting out their seeds. They are not thrown very far. The balsams reach the greatest distance at a little over 6 1/2 feet. Many dry fruits that are set off by touch are also dispersed by animals as the seeds stick to their fur. The wood cranesbill (*Geranium sylvaticum*) has a long beaklike projection that twists as it ripens. It suddenly splits open, shooting out the seeds at its tip.

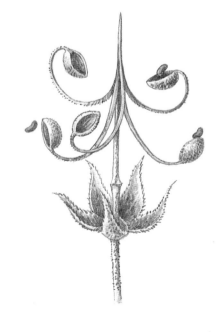

Animal transport

Fruits are a major food for many animals. The seeds are not broken down, but pass out of the animal's gut in its droppings. Fruits are often bright red in summer and dark in autumn so that they show up well. Nuts are collected by squirrels and birds and grass seeds are eaten by birds and grazing animals. However, plants use a lot of energy to make edible fruits, so some have developed sticky, hooked, or prickly fruits. These get caught on the fur or feathers of passing animals and "hitch a ride."

Water ways

The seeds of many water plants can float. The tough fruits of the South Pacific coconut palm can float in the sea for up to four months. Other water plants have oily seeds that can float. The sacred lotus (*Nelumbium nelumbo*) from Asia has large blooms growing high above the water. When the seeds are ripe, the seed holder breaks off and turns upside-down. It is swept away by water currents, releasing its seeds as it goes.

GERMINATION

The seeds of flowering plants are all very small compared with the plant that grows from them. An adult human may weigh 20 times more than a baby, but a mature tree can weigh up to one trillion times more than one of its seeds.

Inside every seed is the embryo or young plant and a store of food. The way a new plant grows from a seed is called germination. To germinate a seed needs water, oxygen, and the right temperature. Water helps to dissolve the seed's food store so that it can be used, somewhat like when water is added to dry soup mix, making soup you can digest. Water also helps to swell the seed and burst the seed coat so that the new plant can escape and grow.

Sprouting and shooting

As the seed starts to germinate, the tiny root and shoot inside it swell. Soon they break through the seed coat – first the root, then the shoot. The tiny root or radicle grows down into the soil because it is attracted by the pull of the Earth's gravity. Soon the root grows tiny root hairs and starts to absorb water and minerals from the soil.

Gravity has the opposite effect on the shoot and it grows up toward the soil surface. Once it reaches the surface, it grows toward the light. This makes sure that the leaves have enough light to make their own food by photosynthesis.

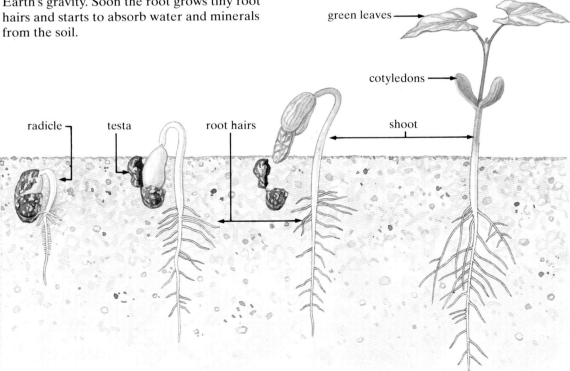

green leaves

cotyledons

radicle

testa

root hairs

shoot

Seeds must be exposed to the right temperature before they will germinate. Some seeds, especially tropical ones like durian and mangrove, germinate as soon as they are ripe. Some seeds have a dormant or resting period and this is often controlled by temperature. Some Mediterranean plants do not germinate if it is too hot. Many seeds need to be exposed to cold before they will begin to grow. They germinate when the temperature rises and the day lengthens.

Keeping the shoot safe

The delicate growing tip of the shoot needs to be protected from the hard soil particles as it pushes its way upward. Seeds do this in several different ways. Broad bean shoots are bent over like a hook, so the stem does the pushing. Mustard and onion shoots keep their seed coats over their heads until they reach the air. Corn shoots have a special leaflike sheath called a coleoptile wrapped around them.

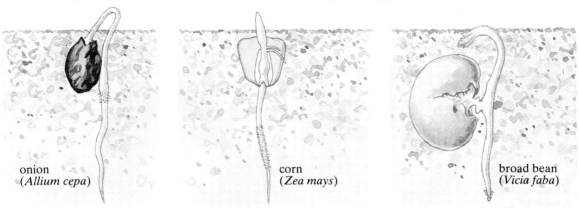

onion
(*Allium cepa*)

corn
(*Zea mays*)

broad bean
(*Vicia faba*)

Different leaves

As soon as the shoot reaches the light, it spreads out its leaves and starts to make its own food. These first leaves, the cotyledons, are often a very different shape from the plant's other leaves. In some plants, like the broad bean, the cotyledons form the seed's food store, and are very fat. They stay below ground, and gradually shrivel up as the seed germinates and uses up the food.

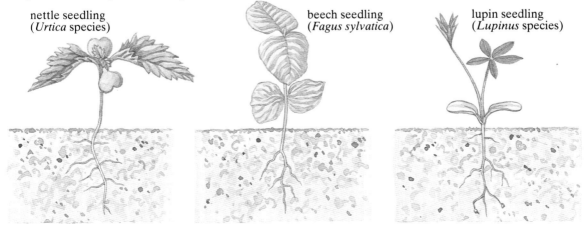

nettle seedling
(*Urtica* species)

beech seedling
(*Fagus sylvatica*)

lupin seedling
(*Lupinus* species)

LOST HABITATS

The plants and animals that live in a particular area or habitat rely on each other in many ways. The ecology or relationship between the plants, animals, and their surroundings is a delicate balance. If you upset or destroy one part of this ecosystem then the balance changes and many plants and animals may be lost forever. Sometimes the balance is destroyed by a natural disaster such as an earthquake or hurricane. Often it is upset by peoples' actions.

As the human population increases, so does the need for food.

Advancing farmlands
The fertilizers we use to increase production of our crops are destroying many of the native plants of temperate areas. Fertilizers and chemicals drain off the land into rivers and lakes, polluting the water, and destroying plants and animals.

Many of the natural temperate grasslands of the world have been plowed up for food, and planted with crops to feed people and their livestock. Farming or overgrazing of tropical grasslands has turned fields to sandy wastes and the native plants can no longer survive. Each year about 45,000 square miles of farmland are becoming desert. However, people are now aware of the problems and much is being done to repair the damage and prevent further loss of our plants and wildlife.

Many European hedgerows, which provide shelter and shade for animals and plants, have been plowed up or destroyed by weed killers. Hedges act as windbreaks and water breaks, protecting the topsoil in fields from being washed away by rainwater or blown away by the wind.

Tropical forests

About 50 percent of the Earth's plants thrive in the wet, hot tropical rain forests. Over 1,000 different kinds of plants grow in just 1,250 acres of the Amazon River jungle. People are destroying these forests at the rate of 100 acres a minute, which means an area of forest the size of Austria is lost every year. Plants no one even knew existed are probably being lost. The forests are being destroyed to make way for homes, farms, and roads, but the plants they replace and the animals that depend on them are lost forever. Often the soil is too poor to support crops or farm animals. The topsoil is lost or blown away and the land becomes useless.

Disappearing wetlands

About 25 percent of the salt marshes of temperate areas such as the U.S. and U.K. have been drained. The soil is often rich and fertile, and makes good pasture land, ideal for grazing cattle, growing plants, or building houses. Many saltwater plants, which created these fertile lands in the first place by trapping mud in their roots and building up the land, are being destroyed and are threatened with extinction.

Freshwater reedbeds that provide food and shelter for many animals are also being lost. The land is being drained and used for farming – the plants and animals that can only survive there are being lost forever.

FLOWERS UNDER THREAT

As the natural habitats are being lost, so the survival of some plants is being threatened. Some people believe that with the loss of the rain forest and other habitats as many as five plants become extinct each day. There are over 20,000 threatened species, and many of these may be useful to people as well as playing an important role in the ecosystem. It appears that for every plant that disappears, between 10 and 30 other organisms (living things) also die.

People are now aware that thousands of plants are in danger and much is being done to try to preserve the green world on which we all depend. Groups such as CITES and the World Wide Fund for Nature are funding projects to help preserve endangered plants and habitats.

Disappearing orchids

There are over 25,000 kinds of orchid and they grow all over the world. Many orchids are very specialized, with unusual flowers that can only be pollinated by particular insects or birds. Often they can only grow in special conditions in very limited areas. So, if the animals die or the conditions change, the orchid cannot survive. Their beautiful blooms are also their downfall as they are attractive to people as well as pollinators. So many have been collected that some species no longer survive in the wild. The military orchid (*Orchis militaris*) pictured here was once common but is now very rare.

Lost Hawaii

The Hawaiian islands used to be overflowing with plants that grew only in that state. As the islands became popular as a vacation resort, land was cleared and large hotels were built. Many plants died out as their specialized habitats were lost and the air became polluted with exhaust fumes. Hundreds of flowers are extinct and many more are endangered. The silversword (*Argyroxiphium sandwicense*) shown here grows only in Hawaii.

Beautiful losers

Many of the plants in danger are ornamental plants that have been collected for use in gardens. Rare species of cacti from the southern U.S. and Mexico are close to extinction. The banksias and "kangaroo paws" of Australia are under threat as their blooms have been cut for resale in florist shops. Wild daffodils no longer grow in Portugal, and wild bulbs are big business in Turkey where about 770,000 pounds are exported every year. In the U.S. some 20 species of bulb are found only in national parks. Poaching is very profitable and difficult to stop. In the mid-1980s, one *Strombocactus disciformis* cactus plant could be sold for several hundred dollars.

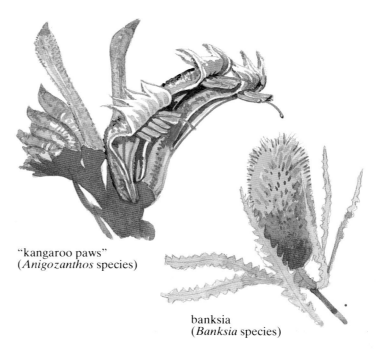

"kangaroo paws"
(*Anigozanthos* species)

banksia
(*Banksia* species)

CARNIVOROUS PLANTS

Plants are the main food for many animals. Armies of caterpillars attack their leaves, and birds and mammals eat their fruits and seeds. However, there are some plants that kill and eat animals. They are carnivorous or "meat-eating" plants. These plants live in places where the soil contains very little food for them, and the animals they trap provide extra nourishment.

This means that the plants can spread and colonize many areas that could not otherwise support plant life.

Plants cannot move, so they have to lure their prey with attractive smells and colors. Neither do they have teeth to eat their prey. Instead, they produce special chemicals called enzymes which dissolve the prey until it forms a kind of soup that the plant can absorb.

A prison for flies

The leaves of the Venus fly-trap (*Dionaea muscipula*) have a hinge down the middle. The center of the leaf is red and shiny, and flies mistake it for a juicy piece of meat. When the fly lands on the leaf it touches special sensitive hairs. This causes the leaf to snap shut. The long spikes on the edge of the leaf lock together like the bars of a prison.

Stuck fast!

The leaves of the sundew (*Drosera* species) are covered in red tentacles, like little arms. At the end of each tentacle is a lump of very strong glue. Insects that land on the leaf stick to the tentacles. As an insect struggles to escape, it touches more and more tentacles, becoming even more firmly stuck. Slowly, the tentacles close over the insect and the plant starts to digest it.

Death by drowning

Pitcher plants have strange jug-shaped leaves – "pitchers." At the bottom of each pitcher is a pool of liquid. A sweet-smelling, sugary substance around the rim of the pitcher attracts insects, but any that land there to feed will be caught. The surface of the pitcher is covered in slippery scales of wax that stick to the insects' feet.

The insects slither down into the liquid where they drown.

Some animals manage to use the pitcher's trap to their own advantage. A tiny crab spider sometimes makes its home in a pitcher plant, spinning its web just below the entrance. It catches the falling insect before it reaches the liquid below, depriving the plant of a meal.

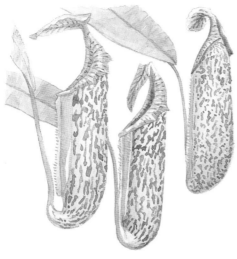

cutaway showing the crab spider

Sucked in

Bladderworts (*Utricularia* species) live in ponds and bogs. All you usually see of them are their beautiful flowers, which rise above the water on slender stalks. In the water below are tiny, feathery leaves and lots of little bladders – tiny bags that can open and shut. At the mouth of each bladder is a tuft of hairs. When a passing water creature touches these hairs, the mouth of the bladder suddenly opens. Water is sucked in, and the animal is sucked in with it. The mouth of the bladder closes, and the prey is trapped.

PARASITIC PLANTS

Instead of making food for themselves like most green plants, some plants have become parasites. They live on other plants and get their food from them. Some parasites such as dodder (*Cuscuta* species) and mistletoe (*Viscum* species) live on the stems of host plants, while others like toothwort (*Lathraea* species) and broomrape (*Orobanche* species) live on roots.

True parasites like *Rafflesia* and dodder do not have any chlorophyll and completely depend on their hosts for food. Such plants often have thin, weak stems, or no stems at all, and their leaves are reduced to tiny scales.

Partial parasites such as mistletoe and lousewort are green and make some of their own food. Mistletoe plants grow on the branches of trees and, as they have lost their rooting system, they rely on their hosts for support and water. They produce masses of sticky berries which are eaten by birds. The seeds stick to the birds' beaks and when the birds clean their beaks on the tree bark, the seeds are wiped off. They germinate and grow into the stem tissue of the host tree.

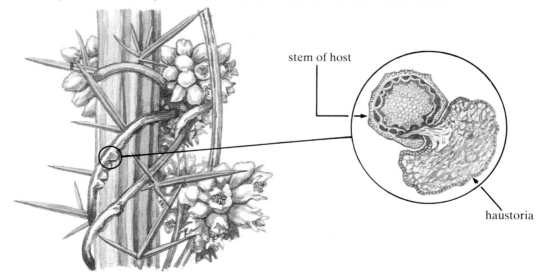

stem of host

haustoria

Parasitic climbers

The common dodder (*Cuscuta epithymum*) twines around the host plant. Small projections called haustoria grow from the dodder into the stem of the host. These branch and join up with the phloem and xylem canals in the host's stem. Food and water then pass from the host plant into the dodder through the connecting "bridges." Once the dodder plant is fully grown, its stem and root attachment with the soil wither away. It is now totally dependent on its host.

The biggest flower in the world

Rafflesia is a most unusual tropical plant. If you looked at it, you would see no trace of its leaves or stem. This is because they are buried in the tissues of its host, usually a vine or liana, from which the *Rafflesia* gets its food and water. All that remains of the complicated structures usually found in flowering plants are the reproductive cells, which produce enormous flowers – the only visible sign of the plant. The flower is up to three feet across and can weigh up to 13 pounds, but it is short-lived, lasting only a week.

Root parasites

Many kinds of broomrape, toothwort, and squawroot (*Conopholis americana*) are totally parasitic on the roots of other plants. They are difficult to see as their colorless stems and leaves grow underground. They are only obvious when they are in bloom, as the flower shoots grow up above ground. Green-leaved cow wheats (*Melampyrum* species) are partial parasites found growing on the roots of grasses.

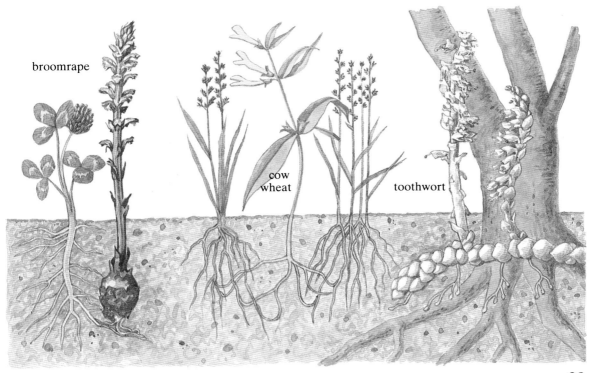

broomrape

cow wheat

toothwort

FOOD PLANTS

Without flowering plants we would starve, for the plants we use as food crops – cereals, vegetables, nuts, sugar, tea, and coffee all belong to this group. People have used and cultivated plants for thousands of years. Grasses in particular form the staple diet of many people, for example sorghum (*Sorghum vulgare*) and rice (*Oryza sativa*) in tropical Asia and Africa, wheat (*Triticum* species), barley (*Hordeum* species), and oats (*Avena sativa*) in America, Europe, the Middle East, Australia, and Oceania. Many farm and pet animals are also fed on grass, both as the green plant and as hay or silage.

Tasty food

Spices and herbs, which are used to give our food flavor, are made from the leaves, stems, roots, and seeds of flowering plants. Saffron, the most expensive spice in the world, is made from the dried stigmas of the saffron crocus flower (*Crocus sativus*).

Fruits

Many flowering trees are grown by farmers and their fruits are used as food. The commercial banana, *Musa*, is a herbaceous monocotyledon. It has a stem up to 30 feet high, which grows from the overlapping leaf bases. Cultivated bananas develop from unfertilized female flowers, so the fruit are seedless.

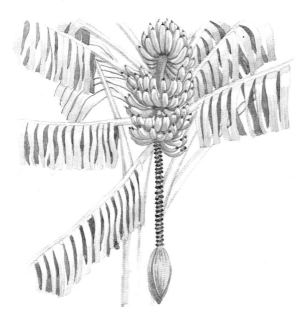

Stored food

Many flowering plants store food in swollen roots or underground stems during the growing season. These storage organs provide food to help the plant survive the winter and to grow again the following spring. Farmers and gardeners grow some of these plants for food and as garden plants. Onions, daffodils, and tulips are bulbs (thick, short stems surrounded by fleshy scales). Potatoes are stem tubers (swollen tips of underground stems) and dahlias are root tubers (swollen roots). Carrots and turnips are long, swollen tap roots.

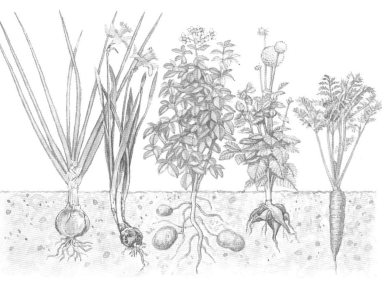

bulbs   stem tuber   root tuber   tap root

Drinking leaves

Coffee and cocoa are made from the seeds of *Coffea arabica* and *Theobroma cacao* shrubs, respectively. Tea is made from the shrub *Camellia sinensis*. It has been cultivated for over 3,000 years and is grown throughout Asia, where it is a major crop. Tea is one of the main exports on which these countries depend.

USEFUL PLANTS

As well as being a valuable source of food, flowering plants provide people with the other basics of life – warmth, clothing, and shelter. The first shelters were probably built from branches, grass, and leaves. A great deal of wood is still used to build homes and make furniture. As long ago as the Old Stone Age, plant fibers were used to make rope. Some clothing is also made from plant fibers.

Many flowering plants provide important medicines. For example, painkillers like cocaine and morphine are made from the leaves of the coca tree (*Erythroxylona coca*) and the poppy plant (*Papaver somniferum*), respectively. Atropine, from deadly nightshade (*Atropa belladonna*) and henbane (*Hyoscyamus niger*), can be used as an anesthetic during surgery and to help people with asthma. The discovery of quinine, which comes from the Peruvian *Cinchona* tree, has saved the lives of many malaria victims. Many people with heart disease depend on digitalis, made from foxgloves. Vincristine and vinblastine from the rosy periwinkle (*Vinca rosea*) are used in the fight against leukemia. Over a quarter of all known medicines are based on plants.

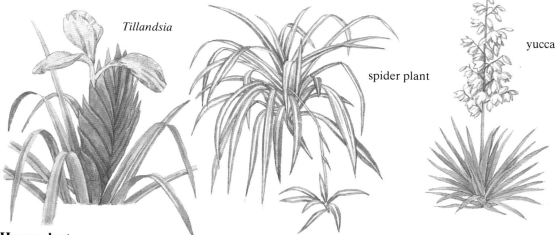

Tillandsia

spider plant

yucca

House plants
Many of the plants used to brighten up homes come from tropical or subtropical regions. Yucca plants from the southern U.S. and South America, the South American spider plant (*Chlorophytum* species), and tropical bromeliads (tank plants) are just a few of these. *Tillandsia cyanea*, a bromeliad from the forest of Guatemala, is grown for its beautiful flowers. In the wild, bromeliads are epiphytes that grow high up on trees in tropical forests. The water some of them catch in their leaves act like ponds and are home to tiny tree frogs and other animals.

Tapping trees

As well as being important for their food and timber, flowering trees provide us with cork, rubber, and tannin. Their sap is tapped off and used to make lacquer, varnishes, and polishes. The resin from a small tree *Boswellia thurifera*, which grows around the Red Sea, is used to make frankincense, which is burned in churches throughout the world.

Cotton (*Gossypium* species)

Cotton fibers from the seed pod or boll of the cotton plant are up to 1 inch long and can be used to weave cloth. Cotton has been used in India for the past 5,000 years and was introduced to the west by Alexander the Great. Three-quarters of the world's supply of cotton is now grown in North America. It is also grown in India and China.

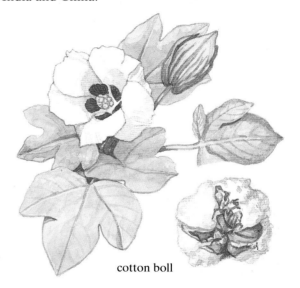

cotton boll

Oils for food and perfume

Many different kinds of oil are made from plants. Copra, made from dried coconut (*Cocos nucifera*), is used to make soap, cooking oil, and margarine. Cooking oil is also made from peanuts (*Arachis hypogaea*), sunflower seeds (*Helianthus* species), soy beans (*Glycine max*), and olives (*Olea europeae*). The most expensive oil is rose oil, which is used to make perfumes. It takes 100,000 roses to make 1 quart of oil.

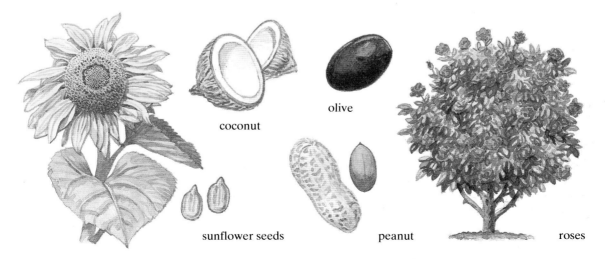

coconut

olive

sunflower seeds   peanut   roses

GLOSSARY

ANGIOSPERM – A flowering plant, whose seeds are enclosed in a fruit.

ANNUALS – Plants that live for a year or less.

ANTHER – The part of the male stamen in which pollen grains are made.

BIENNIALS – Plants that live for two years. They usually grow in the first year and flower and seed in the second.

CALYX – A ring of sepals.

CARNIVORE – A plant that feeds on insects.

CARPEL – The female part of a flower, consisting of an ovary, style, and stigma.

CHLOROPHYLL –The green pigment of plants that absorbs energy from light which is used in photosynthesis.

COROLLA – The petals as a whole.

CROSS-FERTILIZATION – The fusing of a male cell of one plant with the ovum of another.

CROSS-POLLINATION – The transfer of pollen from the stamen of one plant to the stigma of another plant of the same species.

EMBRYO – The young plant in the seed.

ENDOSPERM – The food in a seed which feeds the young seedling as it grows.

EPIPHYTE – Plants that live on other plants taking their food and moisture from the air.

FERTILIZE – The fusing of a male sex cell with a female sex cell.

FILAMENT – The stalk of the male stamen.

GERMINATE – A seed begins to grow.

NECTAR – A sugary liquid produced by many flowering plants.

OVARY – The part of the carpel of a flower that contains the ovule.

OVULE – The part of an ovary that contains the female sex cell.

PARASITE – A plant that obtains its food from other plants.

PERENNIALS – Plants that live for more than two years.

PETALS – They form the corolla of a flower, which surrounds the stamens and carpels.

PHLOEM – The tissue in a plant that carries food made by the leaves to all parts of the plant.

PHOTOSYNTHESIS – The process by which green plants make sugar from carbon dioxide gas and water using the energy from sunlight.

PISTIL – All the female parts of a flower, made up of one or more carpels.

POLLEN GRAIN – Minute grains produced by the male anther which contain the male sex cell.

POLLINATION – The transfer of pollen from the male anther to the female stigma.

SAPROPHYTE – A plant that obtains its food from dead plants or animals.

SEED – The fertilized ovule.

SELF-FERTILIZATION – The fusing of an ovule with a male cell from the same flower.

SELF-POLLINATION – The transfer of pollen from the anther to the stigma of the same flower.

SEPALS – Parts of a plant that form a ring below the petals. They are usually brown or green and protect the young bud.

STAMEN – The male part of a flower made up of a filament and an anther.

STIGMA – The tip of the style which receives the pollen.

STOMATA (singular stoma) – The pores on the surface of a leaf through which gases move.

STYLE – A stem joining the stigma to the ovary.

SUCCULENT – Leaves that are thick and fleshy and store water in their cells.

XYLEM – The tissue in a plant that carries water and minerals from the roots to the rest of the plant.

FURTHER READING
For children
North American Wildflowers by John Kipping; Troubador Pr., 1974.

Plants by Lionel Bender; Franklin Watts, 1988.

Plants by Lorraine Conway; Good Apple, 1980.

State Flowers by Anne O. Dowden; Harper, 1987.
For adults
The Evolution &Classification of Flowering Plants by Arthur Cronquist; NY Botanical, 1988.

How to Identify Flowering Plant Families by John P. Baumgardt; Timber, 1982.

PLANTS IN THIS BOOK

Alpine columbine (*Aquilegia* species)
Arctic mouse-ear (*Cerastium arcticum*)
Arctic poppy (*Papaver radicatum*)
Arctic saxifrage (*Saxifraga nivalis*)
Australian mountain ash (*Eucalyptus regnons*)
Banana (*Musa* species)
Banksia (*Banksia* species)
Barley (*Hordeum* species)
Beech (*Fagus sylvatica*)
Bladderwort (*Utricularia* species)
Blue gentian (*Gentiana nivalis*)
Boswellia thurifera
Broad bean (*Vicia faba*)
Bromeliads (*Tillandsia cyanea; T. stricta*)
Broomrape (*Orobanche* species)
Campion (*Silene* species)
Chaffweed (*Anagallis minima*)
Cinchona tree
Clematis (*Clematis* species)
Coca tree (*Erythroxylona coca*)
Cocoa bush (*Theobroma cacao*)
Coconut palm (*Cocos nucifera*)
Coffee bush (*Coffea arabica*)
Common dodder (*Cuscuta epithymum*)
Corn (*Zea mays*)
Cotton (*Gossypium* species)
Cow parsley (*Anthriscus sylvestris*)
Cow wheat (*Melampyrum* species)
Cowslip (*Primula veris*)
Creeping lady's tresses orchid (*Goodyera repens*)
Dandelion (*Taraxacum* species)
Deadly nightshade (*Atropa belladonna*)
Duckweeds (*Lemna* species)
Field poppy (*Papaver rhoeas*)
Forget-me-not (*Myosotis* species)
Foxglove (*Digitalis* species)
Giant flower of Sumatra (*Amorphophallus titanum*)
Giant hogweed (*Heracleum mantegazzianum*)
Giant saguaro (*Carnegiea gigantea*)
Hazel (*Corylus* species)
Henbane (*Hyoscyamus niger*)
Hornwort (*Ceratophyllum* species)
Jamaican mountain pride (*Spathelia* species)

Japanese cherry tree (*Prunus* species)
"Kangaroo paws" (*Anigozanthos* species)
Lupin (*Lupinus* species)
Meadowsweet (*Filipendula ulmaria*)
Military orchid (*Orchis militaris*)
Mistletoe (*Viscum* species)
Nettle (*Urtica* species)
Oats (*Avena sativa*)
Olives (*Olea europeae*)
Onion (*Allium cepa*)
Opium poppy (*Papaver somniferum*)
Passion flower (*Passiflora* species)
Peanuts (*Arachis hypogaea*)
Purple saxifrage (*Saxifraga oppositifolia*)
Rafflesia
Rice (*Oryza sativa*)
Rosy periwinkle (*Vinca rosea*)
Sacred lotus (*Nelumbium nelumbo*)
Saffron crocus (*Crocus sativus*)
Sea aster (*Aster tripolium*)
Silversword (*Argyroxiphium sandwicense*)
Sorghum (*Sorghum vulgare*)
Soy beans (*Glycine max*)
Spider plant (*Chlorophytum* species)
Squawroot (*Conopholis americana*)
Stinking hellebore (*Helleborus foetidus*)
Strombocactus disciformis
Sundew (*Drosera* species)
Sunflower (*Helianthus* species)
Tea bush (*Camellia sinensis*)
Teasel (*Dipsacus fullonum*)
Toadflax (*Linaria* species)
Toothwort (*Lathraea* species)
Venus fly trap (*Dionaea muscipula*)
Water iris (*Iris pseudacorus*)
Water lillies (*Nymphaea* species)
Water milfoil (*Myriophyllum alterniflorum*)
Wheat (*Triticum* species)
Wild narcissus (*Narcissus* species)
Wild rose (*Rosa arvensis*)
Wild tulip (*Tulipa sylvestris*)
Willow (*Salix* species)
Winter aconite (*Eranthis hyemalis*)
Wood cranesbill (*Geranium sylvaticum*)

INDEX